HE
LEADETH
ME

HE
LEADETH
ME

An Autobiography

DONNEL MCLEAN

WinePressPublishing
Great Books, Defined.

WinePress Publishing (PO Box 428, Enumclaw, WA 98022) functions only as book publisher. As such, the ultimate design, content, editorial accuracy, and views expressed or implied in this work are those of the author.

All Scripture quotations are from the *King James Version* of the Bible.

ISBN 13: 978-1-4141-2081-2
ISBN 10: 1-4141-2081-8
Library of Congress Catalog Card Number: 2011926664

CONTENTS

ACKNOWLEDGMENTS

I DEDICATE THIS testimony of God's marvelous leading and blessing in our ministry especially to Venda, my awesome wife, who was totally with me heart and soul in responding to His leading in leaving the big city and heading out to reach cities, towns, and villages that still did not have the gospel.

When Venda was only about four or five years old, she had been playing in the yard and suddenly came bursting into the house crying, "Mommy! Mommy!"

After settling her down, her mother asked, "What is it, Honey?"

You will never guess what that little girl replied! She said, "Mommy, I want to be a missionary!" Stunning! Right?

Then her mother asked the most ridiculous question, for she said, "Venda, that's wonderful! Where do you want to go?" *You don't ask a five-year-old that!*

Guess what Venda's answer was! It was awesome, and God fulfilled it later in our lives in Japan. She responded, "Mommy, I want to go to where no one else wants to go!" Isn't that simply amazing? *And that's where we went in Japan!*

It takes a very special wife to be a church planter with her husband, for it meant almost endless moves not only from home to home in city after city but also in following His leading to go to every surrounding home in literature saturation. Without fail, she was at my side and inspiring me. In every new venture, Venda never once complained but was always my eager co-worker, adjusting with joy to each and every new challenge. There were times when I was sick—even very ill—and each time, she stepped in to take the helm so that our ministry might continue. Never once was there any indication of discouragement or fear. Her love, her courage, and her support were, without doubt, some of the secrets of our success. Thank you, Venda.

In writing this book about God's awesome leading and blessing throughout our years of church planting in Japan, it is also absolutely imperative that we express our unlimited gratitude for every precious servant of the Lord He sent our way! We owe unlimited gratitude to each one. How I would love to include every name in this brief testimony, but it would be impossible, for the number is too great! I express my heartfelt thanks to all of them and want all who read this book to understand that it was through all their—our—combined efforts that each church was planted and the two new districts of the Japan Assemblies of God were established. To God be all the glory! Thank you, beloved co-workers!

Finally, I am deeply grateful to our very dear friend Donna Sanders for drawing the beautiful picture that is the cover of my book! It reflects her deep relationship with our Savior. Thank you, Donna!

INTRODUCTION

IT WAS NEVER my intention to write a book, but the day came when I knew it was the Lord's will—through dear friends who again and again said, "Donnel, you have to write a book about God's leading in Japan!" And so now in my walk in that journey, with our Lord Jesus leading, I have become even more amazed and blessed as I recall His marvelous provision—always! Each time we really did not have the funds to plant the next church, but not once were we late in the payment of any bill, whether it was rent, the salary of each national coworker, or the printing of our gospel newspaper-tract series, *The Lamplight*. Now, in recalling my Lord's awesome provision, I say with amazement, "He is faithful! He will always provide if we are seeking to reach unreached souls with the message of salvation." Often checks came, too, from folk we had no memory of ever meeting! The thrills never ended! Bless the Lord!

There was one time we laid aside funds to help with the next venture, but when the time came, somehow the funds must have gotten into another account at headquarters! What did we do? Quit our plans? Never! We went ahead as always, and to our great joy again, as always, every need was met, yes, and on time! We praise our Lord! What's the real lesson? If we are taking the message of salvation to unreached people, God will provide! No exceptions! Give Him all the glory!

As I share this, my prayer is that it will encourage others to step out in faith to take the Good News to people who have never heard! God will meet your needs!

So our purpose in writing this book is twofold. First it is to share with great joy and thanksgiving our story of God's awesome faithfulness in His step-by-step leading and in His providing every financial need as we took each step of faith to reach another unreached-with-the-gospel area with the Good News. Of course, we had to be extremely careful and disciplined in the expenditure of His financial provisions. By His grace, every penny was spent wisely and for His glory alone.

Secondly, our earnest prayer in writing this book is that the Lord will use it to bring into vivid focus the millions of people "out there," including those in countries where missionaries are ministering, who have somehow been bypassed and forgotten, as is the case in Japan. We pray our readers will not get so involved in busy and important ministries that they forget those who are still unreached. May our Lord use this book to stir many hearts to hear His voice and to commit to becoming instruments in His hands to reach them with the glorious Good News—hopefully helping us, His followers, to *reach every last person* with God's wondrous plan of salvation. A thousand times, "Yes." Oh, that all who respond to the tugs of the Holy Spirit nudging them to step out in faith to reach some unreached people also experience our God's precious leading and provision.

May our precious Holy Spirit so move your heart that you, too, will be so quickened that you hear the endless cries of those out there. Hear it.

Therefore is judgment far from us, neither doth justice overtake us: we wait for light, but behold obscurity; for brightness, but walk in darkness. We grope . . . as if we had no eyes: we stumble at noon day as in the night; we are in desolate places as dead men . . . . We look for judgment, but there is none; for salvation, but it is far off from us.

—Isaiah 59:9–11

Japan

Area - 146,378 sq. miles

Population - 130,000,000

Japan Sea

Hokkaido

Sapporo

Sendai

Yamagata

Himi

Urata

Matto

Toyama

Fukuoka

HONSHU

TOKYO

Hiroshima

KOBE

OSAKA

Pacific Ocean

Kyushu

Shikoku

1. Susaki

2. Nakamura

3. Shimizu

Koochi Ken

Chapter 1

CHOSEN FROM THE WOMB

HOW IS IT that I find myself writing the story of God's leading in my life? Honestly, I never had any intention of doing it, but again and again friends have lovingly said, "Donnel, you need to write a book about your life, for it will bless many people." Then, totally unexpectedly, one day three different people, all far removed from one another, called and very lovingly yet firmly said the same thing. That really jolted me, making me prayerfully ask, *Lord, is this You telling me to share how You have led and blessed in my life? If it is You, then I will gladly do so, but only for your glory and with the prayer that it will be a tool in your hands to inspire and encourage others, especially young people who are seeking your will for their lives.*

As I quietly sought the Lord for the title of my testimony, Psalm 23:2 powerfully came into vivid focus. These words wonderfully express His story of my life: He led me. No other words better portray it. My earnest prayer and only request of the Lord is that it will become a tool in the Lord's hands to cause you, dear reader, to quietly look back and see how He has led you, too, even though you, like me, were not always fully cognizant of it. Oh, what a blessing to truly see how God's hand has been on your life, oftentimes without your being aware of it. Thank you, Lord.

Doubtless, many of us in utter amazement can rejoice in our Lord's personal word to us, for He says, "I have known the thoughts that I think toward you, thoughts of peace . . . to give you a planned life." And in Psalm 139:16 we read these stunning words, "Thine eyes did see my substance, yet being unperfect; and in thy book all my members [and days] were written . . . when as yet there was none of them." It's true of each one of us. Likely, most of us at the time were not usually aware of His hand leading us; but later, looking back, we can see clearly that His hand was guiding. That's my story, and that's why I am sharing it.

I am deeply moved as I now see that even though I did not realize it, His hand was leading. It seems to me it's true even of my earliest memory from when I was only two years old. My father, a very committed Christian doctor who heard the call into home missions, left the prairies of Canada, and with his family, moved to British Columbia to serve and minister to the Bella Coola Indians south of Prince Rupert on the B.C. coast. I truly feel this was the very beginning of His preparing me for my future life as a missionary—because my dad was a home missionary who was serving our Lord in a very remote and needy area. Even then I was being impacted for missions. Awesome, isn't it?

Remember what the Lord said to Jeremiah in Jeremiah 1:5: "Before I formed thee in the belly I knew thee; and before thou camest forth out of the womb I sanctified thee . . ." That was true of me, and I am deeply moved. That is doubtless true of many of us, though most are often unaware of it then. But it's true. Isn't that awesome? That's our God.

Another of my happy memories was our family devotions each morning after breakfast. After we all sang hymns and choruses, Mom or Dad would read missionary stories, some of which still linger in my heart. Whenever there were foreign missionaries in town, my folks had them over for meals, probably even to sleep. So my earliest memories are of those missionaries taking an interest in this lad. Those were powerful influences in my little heart.

Then, very suddenly, we moved to Three Hills, Alberta, for Dad to enter Prairie Bible Institute. It was a major move from home missions to expected foreign missions in Africa, or so my folks felt then. This was their first step to move in that direction. I remember the family arriving in that prairie town on a hot August day. The very next month a missionary from Africa came, and while showing slides, she said again and again, "These people had never seen a Bible, and they had never heard of Jesus dying for them until we came." There was no altar call that night, but this ten-year-old boy made his commitment to become a missionary and to go to people who have never heard the Good News. That conviction never left me. Always, when anyone asked, "Don, what do you want to be when you grow up?' my answer was, "I am going to be a missionary."

Now, in my old age, as I write my simple story, I can clearly see even back then He was not only leading me to be a missionary, but He was also putting it on my heart to take the Good News to a people who have never heard. I am reminded of the psalmist's words in Psalm 18, when he cried, "As for God, his way is perfect." It is! What about you, dear reader? How has He led you? Without doubt, if you quietly look back, you will see that His hand has been leading you too.

Naturally, way back then I had no idea where He would lead me, but now I can clearly see the path in which He led me and that He really was preparing me to reach the unreached. Although I was not aware of it, that's why He led us to Japan—to take the Good News to Japanese folk living in rural areas who had never seen a Bible or heard the Good News. When I first went there, I had no idea there were cities, let alone towns and villages, that did not have a church. No one was proclaiming the Good News to them! They had been bypassed, but the Lord wanted them to be reached too. That became our joy and privilege—to go and tell them. Oh, how we loved it.

God had a plan. Doubtless our God was hearing the wail of Japan's unreached from long before I was even born. Oh, yes, I know I am ahead of myself in my story, but it is very clear that was where that vision got its start—in that missionary meeting in that tent on the lonely plains of Three Hills, Alberta. God had a plan for my life, just like He has for your life—for every life. Doubtless, as you begin to look back on your life, you will see that His hand was upon you too. In a different way, no doubt, but still, His hand was on your life. Doesn't that cause you to rejoice? Jeremiah 29:11 applies totally to you and to me. Our Lord says, "For I know the thoughts that I think toward you . . . thoughts of peace, and not of evil, to give you an expected [planned—by Me] end. . . ." Rejoice.

Chapter 2

SPIRITUAL ROOTS

NOW, RETURNING TO my family's story, the very next year, Dr. Maxwell, President of Prairie Bible Institute, advised my folks to take definite steps toward moving on to some needy place in Africa, for that was where they expected to go. However, they were in for a big shock. When they applied to the first mission they were told, "Dr. McLean, you have five children, and your wife has bad feet. We cannot accept you." It was 1937, the middle of the Great Depression. Dismayed, they applied to other missions but always with the same result. Heartbroken and in confusion, for days they were wondering what God had in store for them. Happily, the good news is that He had a plan. He always does! Hallelujah!

One day while my father was in prayer, the phone rang. It was someone in Victoria, British Columbia "I am Percy Wills," the caller said. "For ten years I have been serving our Lord under the Shantyman's Christian Association. Every year I visit every churchless community on the rugged West Coast of the Vancouver Island, a very wild and needy area. There is not a church in all those communities, and no one but me is taking the gospel to that entire area of endless miles of rugged coastline. Traveling on my boat, *Messenger II*, I try to visit every Indian village, every fishing community, and all the logging camps, as well as the folk manning the lighthouses. I have been praying for the Lord to send a Christian doctor to come to the very center of that rugged West Coast to be an instrument in His hands to reach those needy people both medically and spiritually. Would you consider coming with me this summer [1937] so you can see the need for yourself? Perhaps the Lord will lead you to come. I even have a spot picked out where we could establish the mission. I will soon be leaving for my summer trip."

Needless to say, my parents knew this must be God's hand. So we moved to Sidney, a town just north of Victoria, British Columbia, on the southern end of Vancouver Island. After settling the family in a rental, Dad joined Percy on the *Messenger II*, and together they headed up the coast. They were gone for five very busy months, visiting countless communities and ministering to people both spiritually and physically. Seeing and experiencing firsthand the unlimited need, Dad had no doubt about God's call. So he sent for the family.

Traveling on a large fish packer, we arrived on a dismal, rainy, November day. I will never forget my first view of Esperanza—just two side-by-side shacks surrounded by nothing but rugged mountains, a heavy rain forest, and absolutely nothing else. It was raining heavily and, believe it or not, it rains about 140 inches a year up there. Nootka Mission was born: two shacks on a five-acre promontory on Hecate Channel, hidden from the wild Pacific by Nootka Island. Geographically, it was the very heart of the West Coast.

It was very lonely for us children. There was no school, no fields or grassy areas. All there was for me and my siblings to do was mountain-climb, fish, and explore in our dugout canoe. My older brother, Max, and I often scaled mountain precipices without any gear. We never thought of danger. If either one of us had slipped we would have fallen to our deaths. Happily, the folks had no idea what we were doing. Today, as I look back, I have no memories of being miserable or unhappy in that lonely, isolated situation. We were always busy hauling water in buckets from the creek or cutting stacks of wood and, of course, doing our correspondence-school lessons. As I now recall those childhood days of isolation, I wonder, *Could it be that even in this arena the Lord was preparing me for days when we would be ministering in areas far from any fellow missionary?* No doubt about it.

Years later, our first ministry outreach in rural Japan was so remote it took nineteen hours to get to our nearest fellow missionary. It meant a very scary bus ride on some of the worst roads imaginable, catching a slow train and then a ferry to catch another slow train, and finally, a faster train just for us to see our nearest fellow missionaries in Kobe!

Maybe I should share a simple but true story about those roads: I went first to Shimanto to find a home and get things ready for the family. The happy day finally came when Venda arrived with our three little girls. Ruthy, our middle one, was about seven. It was a hot July day so the windows of that old bus were open for fresh air. Suddenly, as the bus took a sharp curve onto a coastline gravel road, Ruthy cried out in sheer terror. Totally mystified, we tried to settle her down, thinking maybe she had been stung by a bee. But that was not the case. Crying, and in total fear, she sobbed, "But, Daddy, the bus is wider than the road; we are going to fall into the sea." Normally a child would never notice anything like that, right? Needless to say, the roads back then were unbelievably scary. We really were isolated!

Before we moved I must admit that deep inside I feared we would be lonely—even forgotten by our fellow missionaries. Often I would awaken, plagued by such fears. However, I am happy to say that when we obeyed the Lord and moved in, I never had a lonely day. In fact, to our utter amazement, before long pastors and others came all on their own to help us in our outreaches. It was awesome, even amazing.

But getting back to Esperanza, the epitome of isolation, I am very grateful to the Lord that I never had any bitterness or anger. Zero. I am immeasurably thankful, too, that the Lord had become very precious to me. One of my fondest memories was how blessed my morning devotions had become. That hour every morning before breakfast was such a joy. A bit later, one day Dad and I were chatting when he suddenly said, "Son, I think it's time for you to begin having your own private devotions." I remember the joy I had when I answered, "Dad, I've been having my own devotions now for two years." It was true. In looking back it seems to me that it was this precious relationship with the Lord that kept me from feeling lonely or from grumbling about the isolation. How true.

I often accompanied Dad on his mission and medical trips to the local towns—Zeballos, Tahsis, Nootka—anywhere and everywhere. We even went to lonely logging camps that were completely on logs—bunkhouses, cookhouse, and all. His routine was to take care of the sick first. Then we would visit every home and every bunkhouse, taking the *Shantyman* gospel newspaper. The paper was greatly loved by all, for in those days in those extremely remote areas, the only newspapers arrived every ten days on the *Princess MacQuinna*, the passenger/freighter that was everyone's only connection with the outside world. There were few radios. Now that's isolation, isn't it? Almost always Dad would arrange to have a Bible study or church service in the cookhouse or even in the one-room schoolhouse. What precious, unforgettable memories.

And so again, in looking back, I see clearly how God was laying foundations for my future ministry. Let me explain. Years later in Japan, when the Lord led us to Shimanto in very isolated western Koochi Ken, He led us to edit our own small newspaper-tract series of six, which we called *The Lamplight*. Since no one had ever seen a Bible or heard a gospel message, giving them something they could read was the best way to get the message of the gospel to them. They could read and re-read it until the glorious truths gripped their hearts. It's almost impossible for us to grasp the level of darkness when people have not heard the message of salvation for generations. It was so new and so unheard of that the printed page was most effective in bridging the gap. We could share the message of John 3:16 verbally, but nothing would register because it was so unheard of—for forty generations. The spiritual darkness was appalling.

Allow me to illustrate this with this very moving story. I was making my second round in a village in Shimanto. After stepping into a farm home, I was about to place *The Lamplight* on the porch floor. Since farmers were usually in the fields during the day, I did not expect anyone to be there. But as I was about to leave I heard a voice cry out, "Wait. Let me tell you my story."

I happily stopped and listened to Grandpa Kariya as he poured out his moving story. He said, "The message in *The Lamplight* changed my life. I now have such peace and joy. Thank you. Before you came I was totally miserable because of the wrongs I had done as a young man. I could not find peace. Night after night I crawled wearily into my futon, but almost always I couldn't sleep. Finally, in despair, I would get up and wander up and down the streets, sometimes crying in my agony. My children would come searching for me and drag me home or take me to the hospital. I could not find peace or joy. One day I came home and there was the *Tomoshibi*, your gospel paper. When I read it, it totally changed my life. God has forgiven me, and I have nothing but peace and joy. Thank you, thank you. Please take these to everybody in the village, for there are many like me who are just as miserable."

Looking back, I can clearly see that it was through my experience of taking the *Shantyman* to every home in Nootka Mission when I was a boy that years later in Japan the Lord led us to print *The Lamplight,* the gospel paper that was so effective. Isn't that awesome?

Maybe I should add here that although we did not have the budget to print the paper, we were never a day late in making the payments! It truly was God. We actually received checks from folks we didn't remember meeting! We were learning a very vital truth: if we are taking the Good News to unreached people, God will always provide—even from totally unexpected sources. I still stand in awe of God's faithfulness. Even today, as I recall those glorious but very difficult days, I am amazed, for we never had the funds in our budget before to print the gospel newspaper series, nor did we have funds in the bank to plant the next church and the next! God always provided—without a single exception! Glory to God. Every time we took the next step of faith to reach unreached people, God provided every dollar we needed for rent, for ministry, and for salaries. Truly we can say with Paul the apostle, "My God shall supply all your needs according to His riches in Christ Jesus."

Now, coming back to God's leading in Shimanto, I have to say that it was only after much waiting on Him that we actually arrived there—against the advice of many, for we did seek the help and wisdom of others. But after much waiting on the Lord, He clearly lead us to Tosa Shimanto, the largest city in western Koochi Ken on Shikoku Island, which I've already mentioned. Within days of arriving and before holding our first service, a total stranger unexpectedly walked into our new home and church-to-be. In his hands were some decision slips. He simply said, "My name is Wada. Last summer an American couple came here on their honeymoon and conducted a three-day evangelistic crusade. I was their interpreter. Here are the decision cards. Would you like to have them?"

There is no way I can fully portray with words the joy and thanksgiving I felt as he handed me those decision cards! Truly God had not only led us there, but also He had gone before!

Imagine an American couple on their honeymoon going to such a remote unknown city to hold gospel services. That had to be God. And what a confirmation, too, clearly letting us know beyond the shadow of doubt that we were in His will. We had not yet held one service, and we had precious, young believers there to minister to from our very first day.

Truthfully, I have to say that our only purpose at that point was to plant a new church. That's wonderful of course, but the Lord had much more in mind for us. As I look back on those delightful days, even though we were thrilled to see the new church happening right before our eyes, my heart was very heavy with a burden I at first did not understand. I was in the dark, so I gave myself to prayer; so much so that I spent my mornings for a few weeks fasting and waiting on the Lord to find out what He was trying to tell me.

Then, one day, I knew. I got it. The Holy Spirit clearly and powerfully whispered in my ear, "Go to every person—every home." I'll never forget the impact of that encounter with my Lord! Yes, and I can assure you that that day I made a new commitment to fully obey His command to go to every home in Shimanto, a small city of 38,000, and also to every home in the surrounding towns and villages. That was a big commitment, I assure you. First I had left my homeland, Canada, then gone to Tokyo to end up in this very isolated, rural part of Japan—and now this. But I did make that unconditional surrender and, oh, the joy that filled my heart. Let me assure you that every succeeding day after that, as I was returning home after going from home to home, my joy knew no bounds because I was now fully obeying my Lord's command. No more of those feelings of guilt just keeping busy at my desk with church ministries.

Chapter 3

SURPRISED BY GOD

AGAIN, FORGIVE MY backtracking, but I feel it is necessary to include information that shows God's leading in every detail of my life.

During my senior year at a Christian high school, a missionary from China shared his deeply moving story. He had his family stay in Shanghai while he went inland to prepare a home for them. When it was ready, he wired them to come, but tragically, the plane crashed and the entire family was killed.

That memorable night when he shared his heartbreaking story Mr. Mellar said, "I am now praying that God will raise up many to take their places." Needless to say, that night I stood, dedicating my life to go to China.

The day finally came when I was a senior at Prairie Bible Institute, and happily, I had been accepted by the China Inland Mission. It was then they asked, "Do you have someone you are thinking about marrying?" I did—one of my classmates. But as I prayed about it, the Lord clearly said, "Donnel, wait. Leave that in My hands." I agreed, and I am so glad I did. God had His own plan for my life, as you will soon see. It's awesome to know that He has every detail of our lives planned; and His plans are always so much better. Always!

But in 1951 the door to China closed, as Communism had taken over, and Mao ordered all missionaries to return home. As you can imagine, this triggered a huge disappointment that caused me to pray, *If not China, where, Lord?*

While seeking God's direction, a letter written by Jim Brisbin, chairman of the Japan Evangelical Mission, was read to the congregation by Dr. Maxwell. I was back at Prairie for a visit. That letter so impacted me that I rolled and tossed all that night. The next morning I found myself kneeling by my bed, committing my life to go to Japan! That was right after World War II, when General MacArthur was pleading for 1,200 Protestant missionaries to go to Japan immediately. The nation was open, ready to hear the gospel.

Happily, the home office of the Japan Evangelical Mission was located right in that very town, and they were interviewing missionary candidates that week. Hearing that, I sauntered over to their office and submitted my application to go to Japan. To my utter amazement, I was accepted, and here's the explanation of their quick reaction: the board members knew me from my Prairie days. So in every step, the Lord was truly leading me. I was so, so grateful.

Thrilled, I began itinerating immediately to raise my support. That summer, 1952, I attended the Wycliffe's Summer Institute of Linguistics in Caronport, Saskatchewan. It proved to be one of the most memorable summers of my entire life, for there were only thirty-six students, all of whom were either missionaries on furlough or going out as newly appointed missionaries. What's more, the teachers were Wycliffe missionaries—all but one, Venda Riggs. Since she had her master's degree in linguistics and had taken the Wycliffe courses, she had volunteered to teach.

I was attracted to Venda right from the start, but because of my promise to the Lord, I took no action. I just prayed and had the growing conviction that maybe she was to be my wife. The summer passed, and she returned to Springfield, Missouri, to continue teaching at CBC. I returned to my itinerating in British Columba. Exactly one month later, after sharing one Sunday evening on Thetis Island, BC, I knew it was God's will for me to marry Venda. So late into the hours of the night I wrote her and shared God's leading and asked her to marry me. That was a memorable night, I assure you, for somehow I had no doubts whatever that she would say "yes." Why? Because after I waited on God for four months, He gave me the green light. She was the one—His choice. You can be assured that I eagerly awaited her answer, and happily, it was not long in coming. God had been working deeply in her life too.

Venda also knew she was called to missions and wanted to make the final decision as to where. Margaret Carlow, an Assemblies of God missionary to Japan who had just returned to the United States, knowing that Venda was committed to going to the foreign field, kept asking her to pray about Japan. She reminded her of General MacArthur's plea for missionaries.

And so, one Wednesday evening in early October, Venda skipped supper and went to her room determined to make the all-important decision as to where God wanted her. Using a world map she prayerfully went from continent to continent, listening for the Lord's voice to clearly speak. Finally, although she had some fears, she knew in her heart she would be safer there in God's will than in her mother's home living out of His will. That night, she committed her life to go to Japan.

The very next morning, Thursday, my letter arrived, asking her to marry me. She was stunned and, apparently, thrilled. Her response was an immediate "yes." What joy filled her heart—and mine, when I received that very special letter!

God knew where we would be ministering in Japan, and He knew that in those isolated, unreached areas I would need an extraordinary wife. There would be no English schools for our children to attend. Teaching children by correspondence is not easy, but Venda happily did it and loved it, for she was with her girls every day and knew what they were being taught. We worked as a team. After breakfast she and the girls would head off to the room where their three desks were, and Venda worked with them until noon. In the afternoons they were on their own doing assignments while Venda worked with me. My part in this teamwork was to do the dishes and laundry and make sure the house was in good shape in case we had visitors. We worked as a team, and we loved it. The Word clearly says, "Whatsoever thy hand findeth to do, do it with thy might." We did it with joy.

Looking back, I realize even more how immeasurably blessed I was to have Venda for my wife. She was a totally committed servant of Jesus Christ and became my superb coworker, ready to go anywhere. And she never once complained, even with all our moves. I realize full well that there are not many ladies who could have happily put up with such isolation and endless moving. We had moving worked into a clear-cut routine. That was His path for us—to plant churches in various places. It was totally fulfilling!

Chapter 4

WHY GOD LED US TO SHIMANTO

I HAD SURRENDERED to His call to go to every home, not only in Shimanto City, but also in the surrounding towns and villages. It was a very big venture, especially when we were then only two, just Venda and me with our three little children. "How could we reach so many people?" was the burning question. But totally unknown to us, God was already working in hearts.

First of all, at that very time a new seeker from the local printing company started coming to our new church. We knew that was God! Next, Tsuguo Rikimaru, a graduate of our Bible college in Tokyo who was co-pastoring with his father in Kyushu, felt the tugs of the Holy Spirit to come to Shimanto and work with us in our Shikoku venture. We never dreamed of such a miracle! Again, it was God. Happily, his father, a dear friend, quickly approved. So before long he and his wife joined us, becoming pastors of the new Shimanto church. Amazed, we simply bowed our heads and thanked our Lord. Truly, it was not our ministry! It was His! He was in the driver's seat. Hallelujah!

This was totally God, and an exception to the rule, for it had never happened that way before in the Japan Assemblies of God.

That's a fact. God led them to work with us. That couple with their skills working together with the printer were God's team to work with me in producing our own gospel newspaper series, *The Lamplight* (*Tomoshibi*). We did not have funds in our budget to pay either of their salaries or to print the gospel newspapers. It was truly a walk of sheer faith, and I am thrilled to say we were never one day late in any payment! We received checks from folk we did not even remember or know. Now that is God, isn't it? We learned this vital lesson: if we are taking the Good News to people who have never heard, God will always provide. We saw this at every turn, for in all the outreach ministries in our thirty-five years of church planting we never had the funds ahead of time to handle the next outreach, but *every time* we took the step of faith, the needed funds came in. And so, looking back, I am even more amazed and bow my head in total thanks to our God, who is so faithful.

Almost daily we were on the road going from home to home and also village by village. We quickly learned that if we saw a power line and followed it, we'd find homes. Oh, the joy that filled our hearts because we knew we were fully obeying our Lord's command to go to every home and not just keeping busy at home. We loved it. We enjoyed it. Oh, yes, it was normal to come home footsore and weary, but we were always filled with His joy and the thrill of touching folk with the Good News for the first time. Something happens deep inside a person when he or she goes to countless homes and never meets anyone who had heard the message of salvation or seen or read a Bible! Only God knows how many times I wept and wished I were a hundred people, for I knew where all of me would go—to the millions who were still unreached, or, better said, bypassed by God's people in spite of His command to go to all. Again and again I found myself asking, "Why hasn't someone come long before?" The bulk of the population in these rural areas was old folk that had never seen a Bible. No one had yet reached them with the Good News. Truly it was shattering.

After coming to Shimanto, it was not very long before we really discovered what may have been God's primary reason for leading us to this extremely remote part of Japan. We soon discovered why—big time!

Here's the story: Way back in the hills, high up in the mountains behind Shimanto, was a tiny community of about 200 farm homes called *Oyu*. Month after month we faithfully distributed the series, and I assure you that it was really rough going, for the homes were very scattered and often in isolated valleys and even on small mountaintops.

Then the anticipated day finally came when we were handing out *Tomoshibi* #6, the last paper. This time there was an insert announcing a one-night meeting in the local, battered hall. What a memorable night! The team arrived early, hoping folk would come, but no one came at first—not until after 8:30. Later we realized that it was because they were farmers and had been working in the fields. They had to clean up and have supper and then come. We were very surprised when seventeen responded to the call to receive Christ! Totally amazed and puzzled, we asked for an explanation. Quietly they responded, "Over fifty years ago, when we were small children, a lone missionary came by riding on a bicycle. When he saw us children, he got off his bike and shared the story of the cross, using pictures that we could never forget. We have been waiting all our lives for someone to come and tell us more! When you handed out the *Tomoshibi* newspapers, we knew it was the same story."

I can assure you our joy knew no bounds, and we knew why God had led us to leave Tokyo and come to such a remote part of Japan was —first of all—to reach these precious, waiting souls! It was also why the Holy Spirit so powerfully moved in our hearts to commit to taking gospel papers to *every* home in the entire area, not just to those in Shimanto. Those precious souls had been waiting for decades, and time was running out. Glory to God! He heard the cries of those precious folk for decades, and we had no doubt then that He had led us every step until we had reached them. Glory to God!

Please let me add this: that evening in tiny Oyu was worth my entire missionary career. And, happily, there has been an unending stream of precious souls from that little hamlet who have responded to the call of Christ! In considering this thrilling experience, a compelling question cries out for an answer: *How many other precious, prepared souls are there in other rural communities in Japan who are still waiting for someone to come with the Good News?* That's a powerfully moving question, isn't it?

Frankly, I can't believe there is only one place. Doubtless there are others. Truly, it's of utmost importance that both missionaries and Japanese Christians hear and respond to the tugs of the Holy Spirit. The eternal welfare of many precious souls could be at stake. Our Lord hears their unceasing cries. "My sheep wandered through all the mountains, and upon every high hill . . . and none did search or seek after them. . . . Behold, I even I, will both search my sheep and seek them out" (Ezekiel 34:6, 11).

Chapter 5

"LET US GO INTO THE NEXT TOWNS" (MARK 1:38)

ALMOST A YEAR later, in April of 1966, we moved to Tosa-Shimizu, a small city only thirty-five kilometers to the south. It was a renowned fishing town. Some of their fleets roamed as far as the Atlantic. Pastor Rikimaru was pastoring Shimanto Church and did not need us; although, we returned weekly to continue our never-ending outreaches that included evangelistic services. Feeling the tugs of the Holy Spirit to follow our Lord's example when He said, "Let us go into the next towns that I may preach there also: for therefore came I forth," we moved to Shimizu. Of course, it was another faith venture.

Imagine our surprise and thrill when Dr. Yumiyama, General Superintendent of the Japan Assemblies of God, appointed Suzuki Junko, a graduate of that year, to come and work with us. Our gratitude knew no bounds, I assure you. I here must say that our General Superintendent was from Shikoku, and since no one prior to us had taken steps to reach the area, needless to say, he was thrilled and wonderfully supportive.

Of course, when we made that move to Shimizu, we had not expected help, but once again, we quickly discovered that our God had it all planned. We learned that as long as we keep in step with our Lord, we have nothing to fear, for He always, without fail, provides for every need and sometimes even adds special, unexpected blessings. How awesome is our God! And did we ever love our sister Suzuki, who not only had a keen burden for children but also was extremely anointed. Believe it or not, within weeks there were close to 200 children flooding our little home-church. It was totally exhilarating, not only having precious children coming to our church, but also seeing the fruit of salvation being manifested in their lives. That, of course, opened the hearts of many older folk—especially their parents. Truly, God's ways are past finding out.

As in Shimanto, we did not have funds in our account to cover all the additional costs, but once again, our Lord met our every need. Frankly, in thinking back on those precious years, I am amazed not only at His leading but also at His providing. I cannot explain where it all came from, but every month every bill was paid. Glory to God. Once again we have to say this: when we obey our Lord and focus on reaching the unreached with the Good News, our God will always, without fail, provide for every need.

Every day we were going from home to home, hamlet to hamlet, so another church was birthed. Today there is a beautiful church in that city pastored by Rev. and Mrs. Takenaka, both of whom are from the area. In fact, they have never gone to Bible school. When they first started pastoring Shimizu Church as laypersons, he was told he had to go to Bible school. Upon hearing that and feeling deeply concerned, I went there and found him filling out his application to enter our Bible school. Still deeply concerned and knowing the answer, I quietly asked him, "Brother, during your three years attending Bible school in Tokyo, who will pastor the flock in Shimizu?"

He quickly responded, "Nobody."

My response was simple and very blunt. I said, "Then you must not enter Bible school. You must continue pastoring in Shimizu and get your credentials by correspondence." And that's what they did, both he and his precious wife. He is still the pastor there and is now also the presbyter of the Shikoku District of the Japan Assemblies of God. We are so proud of them and thankful for them, too.

In April of 1968, we moved to Susaki, a city sixty miles east, to pioneer our third church. I learned a stunning lesson at that time. When the time came for the move, the funds we'd counted on became unavailable, but we went ahead as planned. It was a real challenge to our faith, but once again, God fully provided, and the new work prospered. We were so, so grateful. How faithful our Lord is—always!

And He did. Our story is the same—every need was met—even the salary of our next coworker, Obiki-sensei, a graduate of that year. The fact that God provided national coworkers in each place was a miracle, too! As always, we pursued the very same course: while starting a new church, we never ever let up on going to every home in that city and also in the surrounding rural areas. Oh, the endless precious memories, the sheer joy of daily coming home weary and worn but knowing that we were taking the Good News to thousands of precious souls who had never heard.

Then something unexpected began to happen in my heart. After going to countless homes and discovering that no one had ever seen a Bible or heard the Good News, I became overwhelmed with an even bigger burden and sense of urgency. We had left no stone unturned in taking the gospel to town after town and had found that *no one* had heard the Good News and *no one* had a Bible. It was total spiritual darkness—an indescribable spiritual need. Then this question began to haunt me: *What about the rest of Japan? Is it as unreached as western Koochi?*

That led to action, for it was the Holy Spirit moving my heart so deeply. This burden grew, and the day came that I knew we had to take action. That year in Susaki, the Lord very clearly led me to make an all-Japan church survey to locate and bring into focus every still unreached, unoccupied city, town, and village in the nation. It was a huge undertaking indeed and too much for me alone. I had no training in doing such a survey, but happily, our new coworker and pastor of our Susaki work, Obiki-sensei, was both gifted and skilled. What a blessing of God's provision.

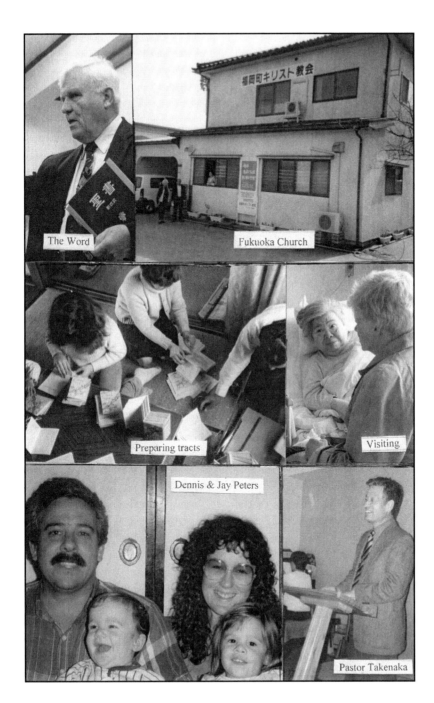

The Word

Fukuoka Church

Preparing tracts

Visiting

Dennis & Jay Peters

Pastor Takenaka

Pastor Inaba

Folk hearing the Word

Pastor & Mrs. Obiki

氷見キリスト教会

Himi Church

Shimizu Church

Pastor Rikimaru

Merian with Gramma Abe

Pastor Kakitani

Just married---in Japan

Susaki Church

Chapter 6

LIFT UP YOUR EYES,
LOOK ON THE FIELDS

ALL THAT WINTER, working together with Pastor Obiki, who loved such research, we made the all-Japan church survey. As planned, using the annual church yearbook, we listed every city, town, and village, focusing on the still unreached and unoccupied. As you can imagine, it took all that winter. After listing all of them, I made a large-scale map to portray the need. I marked the unchurched areas in red and used white for the others. As that map grew before my eyes, I wept, for it was 90 percent red, powerfully showing the vast areas still unreached.

Truthfully my personal objective in doing this survey was to find the neediest, most unreached area of Japan, for I fully purposed to go there. Secondly, it was on my heart to try to motivate my fellow Assemblies of God missionaries by bringing into focus the nation's still unoccupied places. It grieved me deeply that we had always gone only to the major cities. This question persisted: why had we not gone to the lesser cities, yes, and to the towns and villages? What will be our answer on Judgment Day when our Lord asks that same question about the multitudes of precious Japanese souls doomed to a lost eternity?

That colored map very powerfully portrayed the unlimited need of the nation.

Our Lord's own example in Matthew 9 is so powerful. It reads, "Jesus went about all the cities and villages . . . preaching the gospel. . . ." According to the historian Josephus, there were close to 200 towns and cities in Galilee. That's a lot of places to walk to, isn't it? But our Lord did—and on dusty dirt roads! So now He says, "It's your turn. Follow My example." He just didn't command us to go to every person and place, did He? He himself actually did it. I really can't fathom how, for He ministered on earth for only three short years, yet He did that. *Thank you, Jesus. Help us to follow your example and fulfill your expectations. That's our calling—to go to every man, woman, and child on planet earth, sharing the Good News.*

Through this survey, Hokuriku loomed as the neediest and most unreached area of Japan, and so, happily, I knew then where our next venture would be. However, I soon discovered our Lord had another, much larger objective in His leading us to Koochi and the making of that nationwide survey. His ways are past finding out, aren't they? No doubt, from the start, it was His leading to show us the unparalleled need, first of Koochi Ken, but much, much more the great need of the whole nation. As I've explained, I did it also to inspire my fellow missionaries, but unknown to me, God had bigger plans far beyond my expectations.

This was His real purpose in leading us to Shikoku. Is this not what He says in Isaiah 55:9? "For as the heavens are higher than the earth, so are my ways higher than your ways, and my thoughts than your thoughts." How gloriously true.

Sam Archer, the editor of the *Japan Harvest*, a quarterly publication of the Japan Evangelical Missionary Association, and a close friend, upon hearing about our survey, immediately called me and said, "Please allow us to publish it in the next *Japan Harvest*." Very much surprised, I agreed, and it was printed in full color that summer—1970. It included a full-sized map of Japan, too!

Suffice it to say, the impact was enormous, far beyond anything I had ever dreamed of. But then I realized that it was our Lord's ultimate plan from the very beginning. That's why He led us to total saturation in Koochi. He had a plan to show me, first of all, the unlimited spiritual darkness of the nation and then to bring all of that need into the awareness of the nation's missionaries and nationals. Stunned, all I could do was thank Him. Truly, God's ways are past finding out. Hallelujah!

Ten years later, when we had already begun our ministry in Hokuriku, the Japan Evangelical Association contacted me and asked that I do a follow-up on that original nationwide survey. It was a difficult assignment, but when the final survey was completed, our joy knew no bounds, for we discovered that there were hundreds of new churches that had been planted. Happily, many of them were in the previously unreached places.

And what's more, as a direct result of that survey, concerned missionaries gathered to wait on the Lord and seek further direction. At that gathering, the *Church Information Center* was birthed! In fact, to get it started, Sam Archer, the editor, and I personally hired a fulltime Japanese worker to do the original files, listing every church nationwide so missionaries could easily find out the places that still had no church. Truly, we can say, "He leadeth me," can't we? It teaches us a lesson we all need to learn: when our Lord leads us into new ventures, it's imperative that we realize that His plan—His thoughts—are much bigger than ours and, too, He needs our partnership.

Chapter 7

TRIED BY FIRE

ON OUR RETURN from furlough in August of 1971, we were eagerly anticipating beginning our new venture in Hokuriku, called by the Japanese "The Kingdom of Buddhism" (Bukkyoo no Ookoku). But the Lord had a surprise awaiting us!

Florence Byers, a veteran missionary who had pioneered the Shinai Children's Home in Kobe, was ill and called us, requesting that we fill in until December so she could return to the States for urgent rest and medical treatment. Of course, though disappointed, we readily agreed to do so. But we had no idea what was in store for us! It was the trial of our lives, as you will quickly see. Nevertheless, we happily moved in, together with our daughter Naomi. Our two older daughters, Merian and Ruth, were living in our mission hostel while they were going to high school at Christian Academy in Tokyo. It was a difficult time for them that we learned of later.

We loved the children of the orphanage and the two precious Japanese women who ran it. How they loved the Lord! Two months slipped by, then in November, we attended the Kinki District's (Osaka area) annual fall retreat. Together with the older children of the orphanage, we were attending the last service Sunday morning when the phone rang and Kawana-san, the matron in the orphanage taking care of the younger children, tearfully said, "The orphanage has burned to the ground!"

Totally shocked and stunned beyond description, we hurried home and, to our horror, saw the smoldering ashes of what once was our beautiful orphanage! It was a dismal, rainy day. The entire area was roped off, and police were there to make sure no one entered the grounds to try to hide any possible evidence as to what had caused the fire.

Our pain and shock knew no bounds, and we knew full well that in Japan, if you are the cause of a fire, you have to leave that part of the country and appear somewhere where no one knows you. Yes, it's that tough. Oh, how our hearts cried out, "Why, Lord?"

A special team of investigators arrived and for two weeks searched through the ashes to find the cause of the fire. Day after day, standing in the drizzling rain, Venda and I watched the team go through the mountains of ashes. Neighbors were always standing outside the rope barriers watching. Those were the most trying days of our lives. And we had no idea what was going to happen to us or the dear orphaned children, some of whom had already been sent to other facilities.

I'll never forget the stunning words of faith and victory that we kept hearing from both of the Japanese ladies who ran the orphanage. In amazing spiritual victory we heard them say day after day to all the onlookers, including our neighbors, "Our God is the true and living God. Just wait and see, for He is going to give us a bigger and better orphanage. All things work together for good." We were so encouraged by their vibrant faith that was so visible—in spite of the fact that they had lost everything they owned!

Happily, in the final analysis, Venda, who had come to the retreat after the rest of us, was exonerated, for they found everything electrical had been turned off, as had the gas outlets. We were so relieved and grateful. Still the horrible tragedy had happened. *Why?*

The orphanage was gone. Then, too, mission headquarters in Springfield, Missouri, ordered us to sell the property and divide it between the JAG (Japan Assemblies of God) and the missionary fellowship. Heartbroken, I was losing a lot of sleep.

But then, one unforgettable morning, the Lord spoke so clearly. Almost in an audible voice, He whispered, *"Just wait and see. All things work together for good. I have a plan—a bigger and better plan."* I will never forget the peace that filled my heart at that moment. It's just as David says in Psalm 23:4, "Yea, though I walk through the valley of the shadow of death, I will fear no evil: for thou art with me; thy rod and thy staff they comfort me." Hallelujah!

However, since orders had come from headquarters, telling us to sell the property and divide the funds, with an extremely heavy heart, I wrote the toughest letter of my lifetime to Wes Hurst, Far East Director, sharing from my heart what I had heard those precious ladies saying and what the Lord had spoken to me—namely, it was not God's will to sell the property; rather it was His will to rebuild! I had to tell those at headquarters it was God's will for the orphanage to continue and, too, that it would be bigger and better. I also shared what those two precious ladies had unceasingly been saying to everyone and that even university students were standing in the local railway stations collecting money to rebuild the orphanage. But, truthfully, when I was writing that letter I feared I would be called home and even be dismissed from the mission! But I had to obey the Lord and His clear leading, so I did!

At the same time, I wrote to Earl Taylor, the field chairman, sharing my heart or, better said, His heart. You can be assured I was immeasurably grateful when Earl got on board with me, fully intending to fight for the rebuilding of the orphanage alongside me. And, happily, Brother Hurst also was touched of the Lord and understood this ministry was to continue! My final stop was to see the orphanage pastor, Rev. Sugimoto, and share my heart. How I rejoiced when he quietly responded, "I've been waiting for someone to come and say the orphanage must be rebuilt. Thank you for coming. We will rebuild."

And so, after much prayerful discussion, it was decided we would sell half the western half of the orphanage property to the Chinese restaurant next door. And, happily, they not only paid a good price, but also they added extra funds to help rebuild the orphanage. This was of God, a vital part in His bigger, better plan! He was keeping the vivid promise He had spoken that memorable morning when I was in such despair. Thank you, Lord!

With all the funds that flowed in, not only was a new and better orphanage rebuilt, but also money was designated to build missionary homes and to help the JAG complete their new headquarters building that was then under construction. In fact, as I remember it, since the missionaries could do no more to help financially, the national church appealed to their churches across the nation. The response was stunning, and the national headquarters building was completed! Truly, God's ways are past finding out, aren't they? He had a plan, even in the midst of that agonizing tragedy.

Without doubt it was the severest trial we ever had to go through, but now, looking back, we can say that it was worth it. It's when times are toughest that our faith grows the most. The Word never promises to keep us *from* trouble and trials, right? But, happily, our God does promise *to be with us* through them.

Isaiah 43:1–2, 5 says it clearly, doesn't it? Our Lord says, "Fear not . . . I have called thee by thy name; thou art mine. When thou passest through the waters, I will be with thee; and through the rivers, they shall not overflow thee; when thou walkest through the fire, thou shalt not be burned; . . . Fear not: for I am with thee." And in 1 Peter 4:12–13, He also says, "Beloved think it not strange concerning the fiery trial which is to try you, as though some strange thing happened unto you: but rejoice. . . ." And in 1 Peter 5:10, "But the God of all grace, who hath called us unto his eternal glory by Christ Jesus, after that ye have suffered awhile, make you perfect, stablish, strengthen, settle you."

Chapter 8

THE UNEXPECTED

WHEN SISTER BYERS returned in December, strong and well, we moved to an apartment in Tokyo with the intention of making that eagerly and long-anticipated move to Hokuriku at last. All furlough we had shared our dreams with our faithful supporters and now—or so we thought—was the time. But we had another totally unexpected surprise awaiting us.

There is no way I can ever forget the day Brother Yumiyama, General Superintendant of the Japan Assemblies of God, asked me to come to his office. He was a dear man that I deeply loved and respected; he was a real man of God, and a visionary leader. After chatting awhile, very quietly he opened his heart and softly said, "Brother McLean, for years I have had a heavy burden for Yamagata City up north in Tohoku. Again and again I have gotten on the train and gone there. Each time I would take a taxi around the city, and as we drove, I was deep in prayer, sensing the deep spiritual needs and with that, too, sensing the need to send someone there. Then, of course, I would return to Tokyo, very heavyhearted. In my endeavor to see a ministry start there, I have asked others to go, but until now, everyone has turned down my request. I know it is a very big thing to ask of you since you are eager to go to Hokuriku, but would you please pray about postponing your move to Hokuriku and go to Yamagata first instead?"

Hearing his deeply passionate request, I was very stunned, of course. I had many thoughts racing through my mind, but I will never forget that still, small voice deep in my inmost being letting me know it was He who was leading me, even in this totally unexpected challenge. My response was simple and immediate. Very quietly, I responded, "My dear brother, if the Lord has laid such a burden on your heart for Yamagata, I do not need to pray about it. I am ready to go."

Needless to say, it was his turn to be stunned and also overjoyed. What a precious memory, once again confirming that God was leading us. And knowing that, I had perfect peace; I knew He was in the driver's seat. Praise His name.

So we moved to Yamagata. It was March of 1971. As always, we had but one objective: to plant a new church. Our first task was to determine where in the city it would be planted. We wanted only to go to some part that was not yet being reached with the Good News. Our research quickly revealed that the churches already there were in the old part of the city. But in the western area, where it was booming, there was not one church. That's where we went!

I requested a national worker and knew who I wanted. Thank God, we got him, Brother Fuse, together with his dear wife. We wasted no time and went right to work planning a month-long tent crusade in July—by then, only two short months away. Every day we were busy saturating the area with a double-barreled announcement—first introducing the new church and, secondly, announcing the soon-coming evangelistic meetings. We were filled with eager anticipation and thrilled, too, that other JAG pastors in Tohoku fully cooperated. Thirty days of both children's and adult's meetings was a huge undertaking!

I should add a very personal issue that I was facing then: I was ill to the point of seriously praying about returning to America for medical help following the kickoff crusade. But God had a plan of His own—a miracle!

The big day for the tent campaign finally came, and we were excited and filled with anticipation. Believe it or not, the very first night of the campaign God healed me—totally! How we rejoiced! Let me assure you, I was a happy man, for it had been very tough day after day handing out handbills when in pain. Every day I had to return home often, just to rest and recuperate. Prior to this, different folk had prayed for my healing. But it never came until that moment—God's chosen moment! Glory to God!

So a new church was born in Yamagata, the state capital. Praise His name! It went from blessing to blessing, and today, Brother and Sister Fuse are still pastoring there. They have been so faithful. Their son, an only child, is pastoring in Hokkaido, following his parents' footsteps.

Of course, as in Shikoku, we never stopped saturating the city and surrounding towns with the Good News. Happily, other pastors and missionaries of other denominations in the city teamed up with us, helping us to cover much more territory. It was all joy and blessing—such a delightful memory!

In December of 1974, we moved to Sendai to live in a missionary residence that was not in use. That was a happy day, for God was blessing the Fuses to the extent we did not need to be there, which freed us to begin new ventures. My heart was full of dreams of working together with three established churches in the area to pioneer still more new churches. We would be working with the pastors of these churches and their congregations to see it happen. Yes, we were thrilled again to see God moving. Taking the Good News to every home was a top priority, but seeing new churches birthed was also our dream.

First was Izumi New Towns, a rapidly growing suburb of Sendai that later became a city in its own right. Working with believers in the Sendai Assembly, we did intensive literature saturation, which we followed up with evangelistic crusades. At one of those crusades, a young university student attended and gave his heart to the Lord. At the time, we never dreamed of God's plans for him, but after completing his studies in Yokohama, God led him back to complete the pioneering in Izumi New Towns and to follow through in planting the strong church that is there today. Truly, God's ways are past finding out.

Next, once again, the totally unexpected happened! Our Lord had a bigger surprise for us. Truly, it's an exciting adventure walking with God! We'd already begun outreaches in two other places when the surprise call came from Wes Hurst, the Assemblies of God Director for the Far East, a very dear brother and friend. Quietly, he said, "Donnel, would you possibly consider transferring to take over the aborigine ministry in Taiwan? We have thirty-six churches and an annual, short-term Bible school. We have no one to take over."

Can you begin to imagine the thoughts that raced through my mind? Actually, I had previously been there to teach at their short-term Bible school. Also, the aborigines knew Japanese better than Chinese because they had been under Japanese rule for fifty years. Therefore, language was not a problem. Wes knew that, hence his unexpected request.

After praying about it, we felt we should go. So we moved to Taiwan the very next month—January of 1975. We loved it! Those precious, hurting tribal people were so different from the Japanese. At every altar call, all responded again and again, which was so different from Japan. I had told Brother Hurst that we would go, but we would never leave Japan, where the need was so unlimited, permanently. We intended to fill in only until he could find someone who was called to Taiwan.

After getting there, I knew my answer was right, for we discovered that there were one or two churches in *every* tribal village! There was no way I could leave Japan, where virtually every village and town had not even one church, and no one telling them about our Lord Jesus. But at that particular time, the churches in Taiwan needed help.

I will never forget my first trip into one of their remote mountain villages. It was just after rice harvest and had been raining heavily; so mud was everywhere. I finally arrived at the home where I had been invited. Dogs, ducks, and chickens were milling around and going in and out of the house. That's life among the aborigines!

After ambling in, I found only one sturdy chair. Then I drifted into the kitchen, where a tattooed grandpa was dangling a baby on his knees while he stirred the fire as the rice was cooking. The mother was kneeling on the black, muddy floor, cutting chicken on a cutting board that was black too! I shuddered, knowing that I'd soon be eating the chicken.

Suffice it to say, we had our little home gathering, after which we stretched out on the floor to sleep. There was no mattress, just a thin blanket. Suddenly, in the middle of the night, the aborigine pastor sleeping beside me jumped and left; a rat had fallen from the ceiling and landed on his face!

Yes, I paid a price for going into their homes and eating their food, but I am so glad I did. Paul said, "To the weak became I as weak that I might gain the weak: I am made all things to all men, that I might by all means save some." I returned from my first trip with severe abdominal pains, but by the third trip, I was fine. My stomach had become acclimatized.

Another time, after speaking Sunday morning in one village, I headed for our Toyota van to go to the next village to spend the night. To my utter horror, twenty-seven people, most of them adults, were already in the van, wanting to go! They had no idea of the damage it would do on those rugged, gravel mountain roads. Of course, I had to shoo most of them off.

We absolutely loved ministering to those dear, needy, hurting people. They were so hungry, so responsive, almost childlike. How we thanked the Lord that every village had been reached and so many were in His family. Discovering this, I longed for the day when this would be true of the towns and villages in our beloved Japan. Just think of it: a church, maybe two, in every village of Japan! What an exciting dream.

I believe it is our Lord's dream too; but in Japan, we have a long, long way to go. As of now, very few places there have a church at all. Our Lord said it well: "The harvest truly is plenteous, but the laborers are few; pray ye, therefore, the Lord of the harvest, that he will send forth laborers into his harvest."

Finally, after eighteen months of fulfilling ministry, the new missionary arrived, and we left. But we were not to go back to Japan and Hokuriku yet. It was time for an already belated furlough.

Chapter 9

IN HOKURIKU
AT LONG LAST

WE WILL NEVER forget that memorable day—June 16, 1978! It was so hot and muggy that the team headed for the air-conditioned Daiei Super Store to cool off—all five of us: Venda and me; our daughter Naomi; and our two MAPS workers, Pauline Talley and Colleen Dodge. We were missing our two older daughters, whom we had left in California so they could attend Bible school. It was a blessing that Venda's mother lived nearby.

Coming back, we moved into our new home, a large facility Brother Matsuyoshi, a Christian businessman, had purchased and prepared for us. Quickly settling, we prepared for the early July arrival of Brother Uehara, Dean of Students at CBC, Tokyo, who was bringing five Bible school students to help in our kickoff venture. I must say that before moving to Hokuriku we had no promise of help, but our God once again rewarded us for our obedience. In addition to that, to our great surprise, a Japanese lady pastor from Tokyo came with an amazing evangelism bus and her son and two lively members of her congregation! We'd never seen a bus like that.

What vision this precious servant of the Lord had. Except for the very back, all the seats had been removed and a carpet was placed on the floor. (Japanese audiences were accustomed to sitting on the floor.) This was their traveling meeting place that they took from village to village to share the Good News. How they blessed us!

So we had our miracle team! When we moved to Hokuriku, we had no idea either of these two groups would be coming to help. Once again, it was a God thing, and it powerfully confirmed in our hearts that God had led us to Hokuriku. We were in awe and totally grateful!

With Brother Matsuyoshi's help, we had already rented a facility in the heart of Himi, a churchless city of 65,000. It was our first target. Our work was really cut out for us; in two short months, our plan was to kick off two new church-planting ventures in Himi, in Toyama Ken, and in Mattoo (55,000) in neighboring Ishikawa Ken. Thank God for this unexpected blessing from Him! God laid it on the hearts of those two teams to help with this venture. All we could say was, "Thank you, Jesus." He had shown us a plan and provided strong and loving help.

Here was our church-planting plan: the first ten days in July we saturated Himi with the fliers that announced the new church, a first in the city. It was an exciting venture, for there are many homes in a city of 65,000!

Later, the team fanned out again and took the second flier to every home. This second flier announced the first special evangelistic meetings in the new church. It was hot, humid weather, but our hearts were full of joy, for a new church was about to be born. What a privilege to reach people with the message of salvation for the first time. Of course, Pastor Uehara, who had come from the Bible college in Tokyo with a team, was the anointed evangelist!

That was phase one. Next, in August, we did the very same thing in Matto, a difficult city of over 50,000 people. When we investigated, we learned there was a temple or shrine for every thousand people. After arriving there, we heard that two other groups had attempted to begin new works in Matto, but both had pulled out because it was so difficult. That only challenged us the more. It's a stronghold of the enemy, but with Jesus, we will win! Like David of old, whose first action upon being elected king of Israel was to take Jebus, that stronghold that had defied Israel for four centuries (he was following God's directions). Did David know that Jerusalem was the place God had chosen from eternity and He spoke of so much in Deuteronomy? Doubtless he did, for he knew the Pentateuch very well. We, too, felt assured that the Lord would help us take this satanic stronghold—and thank God, He did!

But at first in Matto we were unable to find a rental in which we would plant the new church, so we had to settle with renting a room in the city hall. Happily, there were two Christian families in Matto who had been praying for the Lord to lead someone there. You can imagine their great joy when we arrived to plant a new church. And, thank God, it happened that very summer.

Since we had no national coworker to pastor either one of these new works, we had to carry that load. We shuttled between the three places, holding services and never slowing down our home visitation program. We were kept busy doing this while conducting services in Himi, Matto, and also in Takaoka, where we lived and had weekly services on Saturday evenings. Except for Mondays, which was our day to rest and have fun, the team was always in one of the three places, taking the gospel to countless people who had never heard. Our goal was to enter every home and meet the people in person and thereby find those who showed interest in the gospel. We loved it.

Truthfully, it is very difficult to put into words the thrill and joy of being an instrument in His hands as we saw new churches planted in those unreached cities.

We passionately pray that our story will inspire and challenge many others to realize there are many places worldwide where people still wait to hear the Good News. We pray, too, that the Lord may use it to move many to seek unreached areas and discover the unparalleled joy and thrill that comes when reaching people for the very first time. It's awesome and special! May our Lord inspire many to focus their plans on reaching some of those who have been bypassed by the church.

Again I must say that there were countless times I wished I were a hundred people, for I knew all of me would go to those who have never heard! We challenge you to follow the apostle Paul's example who said, "Yea, I have strived to preach the gospel not where Christ was named, lest I should build on upon another man's foundation." You, too, can experience that awesome blessing. Some are still waiting; time is running out! Please hear this!

When we left Shikoku, the *Tomoshibi*, our original gospel newspaper series, was no longer being printed, for in the meantime, God used it to challenge New Life League, a Christian printing press near Tokyo, to catch the vision and develop a similar and better new gospel newspaper-tract series in full color. That was so exciting! Truly, our Lord's ways are past finding out! This new series is being used all across Japan today, and it was our main evangelism tool in our next outreaches in Hokuriku, too. What a blessing. Thank you, New Life League.

In the next few years other churches were established in the Hokuriku area. The Lord sent Bob and Karen Welch, who were key instruments in pioneering our church in Toyama City, the prefectural capital. Dennis Peters, a MAPS worker first and later an MIT coworker, came and ministered in both Matto and Fukuoka , where a missionary residence was built for us—a totally unexpected event. Today it is the home of Fukuoka Church. While ministering with us as a MAPS worker, Dennis committed his life to serving our Lord in Japan. What a joy that was! Later, as an MIT missionary working with us in Japan, he married a young lady named JonJulienne, who had come out previously as a volunteer. They pastored Toyama Church after the Welches left.

Also, Tatsuo Akamine, another volunteer, who ministered in many places, especially in Matto during some tough times and later, together with his wife, Valentina, started a new work in Uozu, a city to the north. Within months of this venture, Valentina became so ill with a serious heart condition that they had to return to the States for medical help. Happily, though, the Uozu church was established through the vision of YWAM missionaries! Now it is being pastored by a Japanese brother working with YWAM. We are deeply grateful to the Lord.

All of us were involved at the kickoff for establishing Kamiichi Church, a town of about 24,000 that was located between Uozu and Toyama City. The Lord provided a building in an excellent location, but we had to rebuild the entire interior downstairs since it was so old. What happy memories. Ultimately, a young Assemblies of God missionary named Shelley Carl transferred from Hokkaido and came to Hokuriku. At first she lived in the missionary residence in Fukuoka, and later she moved to Kamiichi to pastor this newest church.

I must add another amazing story of God's wonderful provision. To our utter surprise and great joy, Pastor Peter Takagi called from Hokkaido, hundreds of miles north, to say they felt the Lord was leading them to move to Hokuriku and work with us. We were stunned and, of course, overjoyed, for we still did not have a pastor for Matto Church. It was of God!

We had no idea that this talented couple wanted to work with us in church planting. So with delight and wonder, we eagerly welcomed them, but we also knew this would be a critical financial challenge—they had four children! Where would their salary come from? Matto was still an infant church. But, as always, God had it all planned. Pastor Takagi received a letter from a former classmate who had a successful business in the United States. That friend wrote Peter to say that the Lord was asking him to support them with Y100,000 ($500 USD) per month. Truly, our God's ways are past finding out.

It must be said that the Matto work was a very tough spiritual battlefield. Later God sent Dennis and Rhoda Peterson to work with the Pastor and Mrs. Takagi. Pastor Takagi knew English and was an excellent interpreter. Through their prayers and help in working with Pastor Takagi, the day soon came when the beautiful church was built that still stands right by the gorgeous city park as a powerful testimony of God's blessing. It was nothing short of miraculous. God himself put His teams together. We give Him all the praise.

During those happy and busy final years of our ministry, it was amazing how many precious folk God led to Hokuriku to help. The list is long. Everyone was such a blessing. Happily, the JAG appointed a recent Bible college graduate, Hayashi Koji, to come and pastor first at Fukuoka and then at Toyama. What a blessing he and his wife were! His musical skills blessed all of our new churches!

We were so grateful, too, that every year students from our Bible school in Tokyo came, not to mention the teams that came from America to help with the endless evangelism. We also must thank our own daughter Naomi and her husband, David, who filled in for us that one whole furlough. What a blessing! We realize that the Hokuriku District was birthed through the prayers and efforts of so many others whom I would so love to name but cannot because of the space it would take.

I will share about one team from Sacramento, California, though! In 1988, Pastor Ken Bluemel arrived with a team of six on a very hot July day. Because they arrived late, I met them at the airport and took them directly to Yatsuo Town (23,000) that had never had a church. After eating a meal on the local temple grounds, we went to work, saturating the town with fliers that announced the special meetings in a local hall that Friday—only three days away.

The eagerly anticipated day came, and we all expected a crowd at that service. But, to our utter grief, only two or three came! I was shattered, especially since the team came all the way from the United States. I feared they would never want to come back again, but Pastor Ken was deeply impacted by coming to grips with the tragic reality that there was no church in such a large town and that this is normal in Japan. Happily, they came back year after year, as did many others. How we thank God for every one the Lord led our way to pioneer this new district of the Japan Assemblies of God. Sadly, there is not space to mention each precious servant of the Lord who came to bless Hokuriku.

I must add that the secret to God's unending blessings in all our outreaches can be attributed, too, to many days of fasting and prayer. At least two times a year—and usually three times—we had three-day prayer retreats. How we prayed—and how God moved!

Also, the first Monday of every month was always a day of prayer. These were awesome times when the Spirit of God moved mightily among us. We give Him all the praise and glory! His blessings were countless; His faithfulness knew no bounds, for He met every need. Thank you, Lord.

My closing prayer is that our God will use this little book to move many hearts and that many will respond by obeying our Master's final command to be directly involved in taking the glorious message of salvation to people who have never heard. Please don't stand on the outside looking in. He will also use and bless you. Keep eternity in mind. Oh, to spend it with all those you have touched with the Good News! I can't wait to get to glory and be with the many precious Japanese who are there because we went. Many of them I do not know by name, but we spent ourselves unsparingly in taking the Good News to countless homes and villages that had been bypassed by the church.

It's tragic and unthinkable that still today there are people in this world who have never heard of God's plan of salvation. That's our calling—yours and mine—our very purpose for being here. Our Lord's final command, "Go into all the world and preach the gospel to every creature," was spoken to you and me as much as it was spoken to the apostles. That is our primary purpose as followers of our Lord Jesus. When you step out in obedience, you, too, will experience His provision and blessings! Every Christian's life is to be an adventure—with God leading, providing, and using. Find the neediest field, follow His leading, locate a great spiritual need, and take the Good News to every man, woman, and child. With Paul say, "Yea, so have I strived to preach the gospel, not where Christ was named . . ." (Romans 15:20).

Chapter 10

A F T E R   R E T I R E M E N T ,

H E   I S   S T I L L   L E A D I N G

HOW THRILLING IT is to report that when retirement from the field came, God still had a very rewarding and exciting plan for us. As the day approached for us to leave our beloved Japan, I cried out to the Lord, asking, "What do you have for us next? We do not ever want to be couch potatoes!" I will never forget His answer.

One happy day He very clearly whispered, *"Donnel, all your life I have been preparing you for your final ministry, which is the greatest of them all. You have loved deeply, taking the Good News to Japan's unreached and planting churches. Now, in your latter days, your calling is to pray, to intercede for Japan and the still unreached around the world."*

How true! Even there on that field so dark and difficult, besides being so involved in reaching lost, precious souls, I must say that it had also been a long life of learning the power and importance of prayer. The powers of darkness were so constant and fierce that I headed for the hills almost daily to wait on God, crying out for His anointing and for precious souls to be delivered from the terrible darkness. What precious memories.

I will never forget the day when crying out to the Lord for this land of unbelievable darkness and need, I asked, "Lord, what's the answer—your answer?"

Immediately, He pointed me to Joel in the Old Testament, saying, *"Here's my answer—fasting, travailing, and calling His people in every congregation to set apart days of prayer. It's then I will pour out my Spirit in revival power and glory."*

Since that day, His passionate calls to prayer in Joel have burned unceasingly in my heart. That's why, too, since I retired from Japan, He led me to send our monthly release we call *Prayer & Praise Fuel* to intercessors. It was His leading.

He had new, challenging ministries awaiting us, too! Only a month after we officially retired from foreign ministry, God led us through another open door. It was a thrilling surprise. We did not just want to be going to church. Rather, we yearned to be involved in a needed ministry. Well, the Lord had heard our cry, for the very next month, when we were attending a pastors' meeting in Hollister, California, the leader announced, "The men in our local jail are pleading for someone to come on Sundays to share the Word."

Hearing that, I instantly knew it was the Lord's call for us to go! Within a month we were ministering in that jail, conducting services from 9 A.M. until 5 P.M. every Sunday, and much more too. What fruitful, happy memories. How can one forget the times when all those there raised their hands to receive Christ? It's all sheer joy, and we've never stopped ministering in jails and also in convalescent homes, always talking about Jesus. The thrills and joys of ministry never cease. We give our Lord all the praise!

It's on my heart to share something that even here in America gives me deep concern. How is it possible that in a city like

Hollister, CA, where there were over thirty churches, that no one had been going to the jail to lead dear, hurting men and women to Christ? Sadly, that is not the exception.

One day I went to a huge jail, where 4,000 inmates are incarcerated. When the officer heard that I was a minister, he made a stunning remark: "I wish we had a chaplain come here to minister." I was surprised, almost sickened! I longed to go myself, but my home was too far away. There are open doors everywhere!

Another time, I was visiting an injured friend in a rehabilitation center and casually asked, "Does someone come here to share the Word?" Overhearing my question, the nurse asked, "Why? Would you be willing to come?" When I said I would, he called the office.

Immediately I was asked to go up there to talk to them. Excitedly they asked, "Can you come? When? How much will you charge?"

I simply responded, "I can come now, and I do not want any financial remuneration." There are fifty churches in this particular city, yet no one had responded to the tugs of the Holy Spirit to go and share the Good News. How is that possible? That's what we are here for, isn't it? And you don't have to be a preacher either!

The important lesson we must learn is that there are needs everywhere. Each one is an open door, and if we are sensitive to the Spirit, He will move our hearts to respond and enter. Yes, even in our old age we are not shelved because we cannot serve. Now, in our eighties, we cannot express the joy we had in helping in the many open doors we have the privilege of entering. Glory to God! May I suggest that we remember Moses and ask for the Moses anointing? He began his forty-year ministry when he was eighty. Isn't that awesome?

Please understand that there are endless needs all about us! Please understand, too, that each one is an open door for us to enter and touch others for Christ. With that, I bring this booklet to a close. My prayer again is that you, dear reader, will hear His voice and follow His leading. He has a plan for every one of us, and it continues until we go to glory. Hallelujah!

His promise never changes. "He leadeth me in the paths of righteousness for his name's sake" (Psalm 23:3).

SPEAKING FROM EXPERIENCE . . .

THERE IS SOMETHING very much on my heart that I feel should be added to this simple testimony of God's leading and blessing in my life, especially for the sake of any the Lord might lead to also plant churches in unreached places. Oh, how I hope and pray that many will, too. But please heed my humble advice.

First of all, I have to say that hindsight is much better than foresight! No doubt everyone agrees with that! Now allow me to share what's on my heart. During our first very exciting and fulfilling church planting ventures in Shikoku, we truly experienced God's endless blessings. That is a given. But later, in looking back, I realize that moving every year to plant a new church was very hard on our precious children, but I was totally unaware of it! Why was it hurting the children? First, because they had to leave their old friends, and second, because they had to keep on making new friends. In the end, they came to feel that it was useless making new friends, for they would soon have to leave them. That was tough! Oh, that someone had warned me! My prayer now in sharing this is that others who step out to plant churches will learn from our mistake.

Now my advice to any whom the Lord is leading into church planting is this: Find a home in the most central city first! Begin the first new work there, and as the Lord leads, while still living in that same place, branch out and pioneer new works. Truthfully, that is easier on both the parents and the children, as you can easily understand.

Happily, this is precisely what we did in Hokuriku. The Lord wonderfully provided a large home right in the geographical center. We were surrounded by several cities and large towns! So, simultaneously, while planting a church in the place in which we were living, we branched out and planted other new churches.

But if we could do it over again, especially during the years when our daughters were in their teens, we would have found a ministry in the greater Tokyo area so that our precious children could have been at home during their high school years. Since church planting was our lifetime calling, we easily could have found a city in the greater Tokyo area in which to pioneer a new church. That way, our children could have lived with us through their high school years. That would have been a happier arrangement for all of us.

Still, as it turned out, we humbly give thanks to the Lord for each of our daughters! We are grateful for their love, understanding, and forgiveness. And we see how the faithful Shepherd of our souls has guided and is still working in their lives and in the families He has given them.

A POEM BY VENDA MCLEAN

We wait Thy sunrise, God of gods
Upon these ancient isles
Where ebonied against the skies
The temple towers rise.

We know not who Thou art, nor where
Yet all, with aching heart,
Go seeking, groping everywhere
To find thee, if Thou art.

In vain we daily hide our fears,
To smile we bravely try,
Yet 'neath it all our spirits mourn,
Ah, listen to our cry.

From morn till night I till the soil
And wrestle with the sod;
No joy have I, no hope is mine
With which to meet my God.

Oh, mothers all, come weep with me
My baby, cold and dead,
I'll never meet on other shores
My heart knows only dread.

Father of three, I labor long
For meager rice and clothes;
Life's competition, cruel and strong
Leaves no time for our souls.

And I, a grandmother, old and bent
I sit alone by the coals;
For such as I there is no light,
No harbor for our souls.

No creed, no guide is there for me
A youth of twenty years.
Is there not One could show the way
And subjugate our fears?

Masako I—a slender girl
With spirit troubled oft,
The peace I seek evades me still
Oh, is it in the Cross?

Yes, e'en the babe who toddles forth
All eager the path to find
Must somehow sadly learn he's walked
In footsteps of the blind.

Will praying Christians understand
Our muted, anguished cries,
Our silent longings, murmurings—
Ah, will they recognize

That though we know it not, it is
The God they know so well
Alone can fill our aching hearts
And save us from this hell?

And do they know that in their hands
They hold the power, the key,
To stay the judgment hand of God
To set us prisoners free?

Ah, wait they yet, with hearts full fed
When every passing breath
Brings sunset to these jasper isles
And certain doom of death?

WinePressPublishing
Great Books, Defined.

To order additional copies of this book call:
1-877-421-READ (7323)
or please visit our website at
www.WinePressbooks.com

If you enjoyed this quality custom-published book,
drop by our website for more books and information.

www.winepresspublishing.com
"Your partner in custom publishing."

CPSIA information can be obtained at www.ICGtesting.com
Printed in the USA
BVOW07s0644181213

339415BV00002B/52/P